Body Love

Food Peace

Ten Practices to End the War

Terri Leichty

Cover Photo Terri Leichty
Interior Photos Terri Leichty, Joel Leichty
Cover & Interior design by Peggy Sands • Indigo Disegno

ISBN: 978-0-9991448-0-0

Terri Leichty
www.bodylovefoodpeace.com

Printed in the United States of America

TABLE OF CONTENTS

To JoJo, Alé and Laur...
A Thousand Loves.

Introduction

INTRODUCTION

A house divided against itself cannot stand.
~Abraham Lincoln

The inspiration for this book comes from a long and painful battle against my body, alternately using food for comfort and punishment. Through hard work, the war became a peaceful integration of body and spirit, joining to address addiction and compulsion. This work is about a shift; from using food as an emotional crutch to using it as intended... to sustain your life. It's time to treasure your body as the amazing resource and partner it's meant to be.

Fighting with food and hating your body is a destructive combination. Throughout my 30-year career as a social worker, fitness instructor, personal trainer, wellness coach, and yoga teacher, I have been privileged to help countless women on the path to a healthier, happier food and body relationship. With this book, I offer an accessible, practical, deeply personal way for you to begin (or continue) your lifelong healing journey.

Throughout the book, look for italicized stories; some from my personal experiences and journal entries, and others from conversations with wellness coaching clients and friends. I've changed enough details to preserve confidentiality, while keeping the integrity of their stories alive.

The great news: peace is possible! The *other* news? It's a path requiring stamina and courage. Hating yourself and fighting with food brings an all-encompassing, fierce misery. Healing requires embarking on a deeply spiritual journey toward your highest, best, *real* self. The pain of continuing on the path of addiction and body hatred far exceeds the pain of finding your way home. Author Gary Zukav says it beautifully in *Soul to Soul: Communications from the Heart*:

There comes a time when the pain of continuing exceeds the pain of stopping. Slowly, the realization emerges that the choice to continue what you have been doing is the choice to live in discomfort, and the choice to stop what you have been doing is the choice to breathe deeply and freely again.

During the crazy-making years of craving and binging, mind games and hating my body, I knew there had to be another way. Deep within, a quiet voice assured me I wasn't meant to live in this agony. I had long suspected a larger purpose lay buried in my misery. I didn't need the crazy amounts of food I was consuming, but I obviously needed *something*.

My healing journey began with a tentative conversation. Rather than cursing my seemingly insatiable hunger, I decided to welcome it, asking, "What can I give you, instead of food?" I practiced sitting in the midst of the craving; feeling it, but not feeding it. In the beginning, I managed only a few minutes.

A comforting secret hid in my practice: Allowing my feelings to surface didn't kill me. At some point, I had gotten the impression they might. They *did* hurt like hell, and at times made me feel crazy and out of control. But, in the end I realized they had come to serve me; to *save* me.

There's an inevitable crossroads on the food and body journey: continue living in pain, or do the work leading to peace. Take a moment to consider this, because it *is* a choice. You can continue striving and searching for the perfect body, the right diet, or a magical exercise program that will fix what's supposedly wrong with you. Or, you can dive deeper and finally heal the actual root of your pain. Guess what? It has nothing to do with food *or* your body.

This book is about one absolute Truth:

Ending the food and body war is about loving yourself right now, without changing anything.

Sit with this idea, because it's a tough one to grasp. We think we'll love ourselves *after* we lose weight, firm our thighs or stop binging. We've been led to believe a smaller clothing size equals bigger worth. We think no one else can truly love us like this.

Waiting to love yourself until you change your body is about as effective as a parent waiting to love their kids until they stop misbehaving. You must commit to loving your body so fully and unconditionally, you can't fathom harming it with unhealthy behaviors and disparaging words.

Hating yourself is extremely damaging. Your body and spirit wither from the neglect, just as any living organism deprived of love will do. You must harness fierce loyalty and a sense of protectiveness; the same kind you would excavate to help someone you love. Self-love is a *verb*; it requires daily action, and this gets easier with practice.

It's time to expose the pervasive and destructive myth that your physical appearance defines your worth. You are a unique, beautiful soul living inside an amazingly resourceful body. Your appearance cannot possibly define you, with all the unique gifts and abilities you offer. The diet industry, Madison Avenue, and the media sell a lucrative and powerful fairy tale, extremely convincing in its untruth. In Chapter 12, I give you practical ways to stop drinking their poisonous Kool-Aid.

Your relationship with your body is like any other. Without a foundation of trust, communication gets stifled. As you start tuning in to your body's messages, you will understand what it truly needs.

This journey is lonely and isolating. We feel embarrassment and shame that food means this much. We have a deep longing to be understood without judgment. We need reassurance and hope that there is a life beyond craving, binging and misery.

I've made many discoveries through trial and error, growth and lessons. What I know for sure: within your pain lies the opportunity for profound self-love and peaceful coexistence with food.

Long ago, I decided to embrace this food and body expedition as my greatest teacher. Through these pages, I invite you to do the same.

Introduction

Chapter 1

How It Began

Body Love | Food Peace

HOW IT BEGAN

I'm six, and I have a pack of gum, just for me. I press my little nose to the package, hungrily inhaling the scent of spicy cinnamon. Next, I follow a carefully compulsive ritual. I remove every wrapper, and place the pieces inside a plastic egg left over from my Easter basket. I devour my treat within minutes, unable to think of anything else until I've chewed and quickly discarded every piece.

I was a skinny, highly energetic and extremely sensitive child. My emotions were always on edge, ready to spill and create a problem. My parents, weary from raising three daughters before me, had little energy or tolerance for my over-the-top expressiveness. I had difficulty making friends, and was a frequent target for bullying and teasing at school. Believing I was a truly bad kid, I spent much of my time alone in my bedroom, the backyard apple trees, or the make-believe tent world I created in our basement with old sheets and a ping pong table.

My gum obsession repeated like a tired spin cycle throughout my childhood, with food serving as my validator and friend. I worked hard to become the quiet, nice kid everyone seemed to wish for.

It is after school, on a spring day like any other. I'm walking to track practice when a passing teacher exclaims, "Wow, you're really getting some hips on you!" Her tone of voice clearly indicates the lack of compliment. My face flames as I hurry by her, pulling at my shorts in an attempt to hide my suddenly hideous 13-year-old body. My life shifts dramatically, the unfamiliar sensation of body-shame coursing through me. My emotional pain has found a home.

Until this moment, my body and I were partners. I'd always been athletic, loving my body for its ability to run fast and jump high. The teacher presented a new perspective. Perhaps molding my body into a more pleasing form would bring the acceptance I craved.

The next 30 years brought a desperate search for a perfectly sculpted physique. A dysfunctional marriage of addiction and body hatred played me like a puppet in a relentlessly exhausting dance. My high school and college years were a blur of dieting and binging, then purging through intense exercise. I was in a torturous place; out of control, lonely and despising myself. Exercise kept my weight from skyrocketing, but I gained just enough to further increase my self-hatred.

I head to the college dining hall after enduring the daily 2+ hours of collegiate basketball practice. In the next hour, I will mindlessly eat more than enough to make up for it. I don't know what being full feels like; it doesn't occur to me to notice. While I eat, I'm thinking of seconds. I fantasize about the bowl of ice cream waiting for dessert. I've earned it, I reason, with my long hours of exercise. My love affair with food is full-blown, out of control. I can think of little else.

A fast forward to life after college found me married very young, with no insight into my real needs or ability to effectively communicate emotion. The preoccupation with my body and food increased. Armed with a social work degree, I found my first job working in an addictions treatment program. My work brought the first of many epiphanies on this journey. I saw myself in my patients and their intense, out of control cravings. I deeply understood relapse; for them, on alcohol and drugs; for me, on food. I had a glimpse into my own agonizing behavior and was strangely comforted. I no longer felt alone in my anguish.

"I figure if I just eat carrots and celery when I feel like binging, at least I won't do any damage," the young patient states. Without thinking, I respond, "The damage isn't about what you eat. The damage comes from trying to fill the void with food. The carrots and celery are still a binge. You have to identify what it is you really need." The room falls silent; all members of the group therapy session wait for her response. She stares blankly at me, not getting it. She's not ready.

My response rose from a wisdom deep within; one I didn't know existed. It would be years before I could integrate this epiphany into meaningful action, but it was the spark.

I continued manipulating food and exercise in an ongoing, desperate attempt to attain perfection. I transitioned into a career in the fitness industry, diligently learning everything I could about weight loss and fitness. Within eight years, I was certified in group fitness instruction, advanced personal training, and wellness coaching. I was teaching over 10 classes a week, training dozens of clients, and exercising intensely on my own. I continually researched nutrition and weight loss, consuming every related book and magazine I could find.

My intentions were good. I believed weight loss and better fitness was the answer for everyone, but self-redemption remained my secondary motivation. I loved my work and clients, but I also loved what the excessive exercise did to my body. It didn't matter how thin I got, how fit my thighs were or how close my hips came to the standard referenced by that teacher long before. I still weighed myself obsessively, studied myself from every angle and agonized over perceived flaws. An imperfect body meant an imperfect *me*. There was no compromise.

My food obsession increased. It served as comfort, friendship, and emotion-suppressor extraordinaire. I put on a happy face; still the nice girl striving to be helpful, supportive, and empathetic. I rarely expressed anything, especially anger. I reached a safe emotional flat line, and stayed there for many years.

My religious upbringing taught me that when things get bad, you get on your knees. So, here I was, beside my bed, praying for relief. The relentless, exhausting pain of fighting with food, hating myself and feeling worthless was taking its toll. I woke each day to intense fear of overeating, and fell asleep berating myself for my weakness.

Answers and relief finally came through the hard work of facing my deeply buried emotions. This meant halting emotional eating long enough to actually *feel*. I began to face everything, and for a while things got really painful. But, as I slowly peeled away the layers of emotional muck, I glimpsed the beautifully expressive little girl I had left behind, cowering under the weight of my unrealistic expectations, waiting to see if I would come back for her.

Progress, healing, and growth required learning to love myself as I am today. Any change I've made has been successful only when born out of fierce self-love.

Each step also meant learning to be still and simply *feel*. My emotions were trying desperately to communicate with me; to tell me what I *really* needed. This was the beginning point of a conscious, awakened relationship with my body, and started my journey to peace.

Food has been my greatest teacher and largest foe. I have cursed it, loved it, railed against it and binged on it. I've felt suicidal over it, and wept at my powerlessness to control it. Throughout much of my life, I awakened thinking about food, and fell asleep obsessing over my intake of it.

38 years after a snide comment about the size of my hips, I finally feel (on most days) the sweet peace of self-acceptance. The days I don't, I take a deep breath and practice everything I've learned. Lather, rinse, repeat…lifelong.

There *is* hope, and a way to turn your suffering into remarkable, life-changing joy. While the recovery road can get bumpy at times, I promise you, it's worth it.

Chapter 2

THE PRACTICES

THE PRACTICES

W*hat would your life be like if you learned how to respect your body as though it were a precious creation—as valuable as a beloved friend?*
~*Christiane Northrup*

Learning to love yourself leads to finally living in peace, free of food and body obsession. From this place, healthy behaviors flow with ease. Your body can find equilibrium and a healthier weight without the usual compulsion and strain.

It is impossible to make peace with food until you

make peace with your body. When you hate your body, you become a fragmented being, made of bits and pieces of untouched stuff; things filed away as too difficult to handle in the moment. This journey is about uncovering and healing the fragments, gradually allowing you to become a healthier whole.

The lessons you discover in the unearthed layers will bring both great angst *and* untold joy. You'll feel like giving up at times, and wonder why you ever started down this path. Just remember...this path found *you*. No one asks to be at war with food and their body. Stuck behaviors, beliefs and habits take effort, patience and time to transform into a new normal.

Your body serves as home for everything making up your True Self: your hopes, dreams, passions, skills, personality, and beliefs. Keeping it in good health is essential; it's impossible to live out your divine life purpose in a sick, unhealthy body.

Goals based on changing your outward appearance won't help you become your highest, best, *real* self. I spent much of my life with a laser-like focus on getting a perfect physique, while my soul starved from neglect.

One of many epiphanies came the day I couldn't name any hobbies other than exercise. A much bigger one came when I had to survive an excruciating divorce, bringing me more heartache than I had ever thought possible. I was dealing with off-the-chart pain of betrayal, guilt, shame, fear, grief, shock and loss. Surviving this difficult time meant releasing the need to control and change my body, and instead opening my heart to being vulnerable like never before. The balance of caring for my physical and spiritual needs shifted to a more healthy, life-giving place.

The Body Love, Food Peace journey guides you

through Ten Practices. A Core Truth defines the lesson of each Practice, while an integration section at the end of each chapter gives practical ways to work at the healing process. *I urge you to make the integrations your top priority!* This journey is about taking action, not simply gathering information. To make long term changes, you must dive in and apply what you're learning.

The Ten Practices

1. *Ditch the weight loss goal*

2. *Get honest*

3. *Sit with your cravings*

4. *Feel your binges*

5. *Deal with your shadow*

6. Find moderation and balance

7. Learn to play

8. Mother yourself

9. Learn to be still

10. Ditch the scale, magazines, and mirrors

Throughout the book, I remind you to pause and take deep breaths from your belly. Learning to breathe properly (and remembering to do it!) helps to manage the level of stress in your body. Why is this is so important? When you breathe from your belly, you fill the lower lobes of your lungs, triggering what's called the parasympathetic nervous system, or PNS. It's the job of the PNS to calm and relax you. It reassures your body and brain that all is well. Most of us habitually take shallow chest breaths, which fill the *upper* lobes of the lungs, triggering the sympathetic nervous system (SNS). This is the fight-or-flight staging area, where stress hormones like adrenaline and cortisol are readying for battle. They're very handy when you need to swiftly react to an actual crisis, like being chased or threatened.

According to Donna Jackson Nakazawa, author of *The Last Best Cure*, our bodies are supposed to release these stress hormones through physical exertion, like fighting or fleeing. Since modern-day life doesn't typically require either response, the hormones go unused and build up over time. Unfortunately, their chronic presence is known to lead to a range of health issues, including depression, insomnia, poor digestion and weight gain. Cortisol is also known as a fat-storage hormone, meaning it tells your body to hang onto extra weight, just in case there's an emergency in the future.

Traits for Success

To find success on this path to peace, you need to dig deep and harvest the following traits:

Stubbornness – Refuse to accept pain as the norm for your life.

Righteous anger – Reject the perfect-body myth bombarding you with messages of "not good enough." It's time to take back your power!

Voraciousness – Read and absorb inspirational material, but ignore the stuff about weight loss, superficial beauty or fitness (More on this in Chapter 12).

Courage – Face the stuff you've avoided. Have the tough conversations required for healing. Get help if it's too much to handle on your own.

Persistence – Relentlessly question what you and your body truly need in any given moment.

Patience – Accept that the answers may not come immediately, or in the way you expect.

Willingness – Feel whatever emotions come up, and practice locating them in your body.

Unconditional acceptance – Love and appreciate your body right now, allowing no exceptions or excuses. Set the weight loss goals aside (Chapter 3). Your body adjusts on its own when you listen to and care for it.

Open-mindedness – Give up the use of mirrors and the scale (Chapter 12). These external measures of worth are simply another way to judge and demean your body.

Let's dive in by looking more closely at our first Practice: Drop the weight loss goal.

Deep, nourishing belly breath...*you can do this.*

_____

_____

_____

_____

_____

_____

_____

_____

_____

_____

_____

_____

_____

_____

The Practices

_____

_____

_____

_____

_____

_____

_____

_____

_____

_____

_____

_____

_____

_____

_____

_____

_____

_____

_____

_____

_____

_____

_____

_____

_____

_____

The Practices

_____

_____

_____

_____

_____

_____

_____

_____

_____

_____

_____

_____

_____

_____

Chapter 3

Practice One

Ditch the Weight Loss Goal

DITCH THE WEIGHT LOSS GOAL

The woman is about 35 or so. She wears a skimpy black bikini, completely indifferent to the rolls and cellulite adorning her body. I watch in wonder from my nervous perch on a beach towel, where I'm trying to garner enough courage to shed my cover-up. She frolics, runs and plays with her children, not the least bit concerned with the jiggles and ripples of her body. Her laughter dances on the breeze...carefree and happy. Without a doubt, she is the most beautiful woman I've ever seen. I ache with longing to have what she has.

Recently, I was greeted by an email announcing a new book about food addiction. The author has a

Ph.D. which, according to the publisher, made her a unique expert on how to best deal with this issue. Upon exploring further, however, I was dismayed to discover yet another book focused on weight loss.

I get it. When you're carrying extra weight, it's hard to think of anything else. My own discovery, after many years of dieting and desperate weight loss attempts, is that focusing on weight as the problem continues the damaging mindset that you are flawed and must be fixed. When you believe your weight holds this much power, your decisions come from a defeated and desperate place. Food remains your nemesis; something you must conquer instead of befriending. To heal your wounded soul, you must first adopt an unconditional self-love practice. Brace yourself; unconditional self-love means many things, including *accepting your current weight.*

I know this is a tough one to grasp. I know too well the

feeling of fear that arises, with all its accompanying messages:

"If I don't stay on top of this, I will just keep gaining."

"I am unhealthy at this weight."

"I feel (or look) awful at this weight."

"I hate myself at this weight."

"When I'm not on a diet, I just lose control. I can't stop eating."

I've been there, and struggled with every one of these (and other) terrifying thoughts. But the time has come to get honest and answer this question:

How has staying on the weight loss track helped you thus far, other than making you feel depressed, lonely, frustrated, out of control, deprived and resentful?

Add the likelihood you've lost and regained weight (plus some) countless times, and the old way of doing things doesn't add up. These are the emotions and experiences leading to food obsession; those moments when you say, "Screw it" and eat everything you've told yourself you can't have, and hate yourself even more.

Our Practice One Truth:

Weight normalization happens naturally when you step off the weight loss train, affirm your existing strengths, listen to your real needs and respond in kind.

Notice I said weight n*ormalization*. If you're like me, you've been on a diet for much of your life. While dieting is typically focused on reaching a weight you think you *should* be, weight normalization means gradually reaching a weight that brings increased health, energy, vitality and ease of movement. It may not be the number you've been led to believe is right for you. (See Chapter 10 for how to ditch the scale and start listening to your body.)

Take a moment to imagine your life without the albatross of weight loss worry and angst. While it can feel very scary to release something so familiar; relief, excitement, and joy wait in its place, with the eventual reward of living at a comfortable, healthy weight.

So, how does life without a weight loss goal work, exactly? Let's take a look.

Some years ago, three wellness coaching clients posed variations of the same question: "I set my goals, meet them for a while, and then suddenly quit trying. What's wrong with me?" My response to each of them: "What's wrong with your *goals*?"

Most goals are negative, based on *shoulds* and *shortcomings*. For instance, we should exercise, eat more vegetables and less sugar, drink more water, be less stressed. The shoulds never excite or motivate you for the long term, because they come from external expectations. Remember...you're trying to forge your way *inward*...to meet the real you. When you discover what really appeals to you, you'll find a way to get it done.

When goals are based on your supposed short-comings, meaning what's *wrong* with you (inherent to weight loss goals, by the way), you can't feel up to the task. It's tough to find motivation and self-confidence when feeling like damaged goods. All change is rooted in courage, tenacity and, most importantly, belief in yourself.

Start by identifying one or more non-dieting self-care goals that pique your interest. I've had clients set creativity goals related to everything from scrapbooking to clothing design. Others have preferred active goals like learning to ski, attending yoga, or completing a 5K walk or run. When the choice feels right, you experience animation in your body and motivation to take the next steps.

What do *you* think you need right now? You probably don't often stop to ask yourself this question. Most of us rely heavily on outside experts. Great advice is plentiful and useful, but only you know what really charges you up. If an expert tells you to hit the weight room 3 times a week but you'd rather go play on a rock climbing wall, or climb on the jungle gym with your kids, go for it! You'll build strength in your legs and upper body, which is the purpose of a formal strength training routine anyway. You'll have a lot more fun and be more likely to stick with it if you've made the choice. (See Chapter 9 for a deeper dive into exercise as play.)

Becoming your own expert builds *self-efficacy*, an essential component of self-love. Self-efficacy means you believe in your ability to make good choices and take care of yourself. Without this trait, you keep valuing the guidance of others over your own innate wisdom, with continued short-term results. If you can't trust yourself, how will you learn to love yourself? Without self-efficacy, long-term change is unlikely.

Take a moment to remember being a kid...running, climbing, jumping and riding bike. You likely didn't ask someone which part of the playground you should try first. You just ran headlong toward whatever looked fun! Perhaps you scraped your knee or bumped your head. You didn't berate yourself for making a mistake, or ask someone what you should do next. You wiped off your scraped knee, and ran excitedly to try something else. It's fun to recapture that spirit of adventure and discovery as an adult!

I'm 8, and it's recess time. I burst through the double metal doors, momentarily blinded by the bright Colorado sun. I race to the playground, my legs pumping as fast as I can make them go. My heart feels ready to burst from my chest with excitement. Before me lies 20 glorious minutes of exploration.

The day I describe above is grooved in my memory. Despite countless recess breaks over the years, my awareness that day was clear and alert. I can still feel the unadulterated joy of that moment. Anything involving physical movement was (and is) my thing. Maybe you can relate, or perhaps a quiet, creative activity gets your juices flowing. It doesn't matter. When you allow space for your passions, the blossoming begins. You feed your interests, get to know yourself on your terms, and are less likely to define yourself by how you look or what you weigh. You'll also have less need to eat emotionally, go on a new diet, or engage in other destructive habits.

The healing begins by getting acquainted with yourself, a bit at a time. Try something, notice how it feels, and move on if it's not quite what you hoped.

As you experiment, notice your inner critic. She's the part of you who wants to protect you from embarrassment or doing something wrong. If she's driving your choices, sit down and have a talk. Really. Sit quietly, and enjoy a couple of deep belly breaths. See if she's creating a physical sensation somewhere in your body (For instance, I usually feel my inner critic in my solar plexus.) Let her know you're willing to try new things and even make mistakes. Be sure to thank her for her protective efforts...she means well. But, firmly reassure her *you've got this*.

Remember...you're trying to bring the fragments of yourself back to a cohesive whole. If you reject any part of yourself; inner critic included, that part remains unacceptable and shamed. You will continue striving to fill yourself from the outside (like with food), when what you really need is to go inward, welcoming all the parts you've rejected. Imagine a mother, gathering her children into her loving arms. This is you...welcoming all pieces of yourself back to a loving, accepting home.

INTEGRATE:

1 Close your eyes and imagine life without weight loss worry. Invite the Truth that you are just right, right now. Notice the feelings that arise, without judgment. Just notice and feel. Journaling about your experience further integrates this feeling of birthing self-acceptance.

2 Identify a very specific, manageable self-care goal (unrelated to weight loss) that gets you excited. Forget rules and guidelines. Grab your calendar and place the activity on your schedule one time in the next week. Once you're feeling more confident in your ability to meet a goal, any goal, others can be added. You'll get that kick-ass feeling of Wow! I CAN do this! and feel motivated to do more.

3 When the inner critic comes up, practice thanking her and giving reassurance. Journaling

or writing her a letter helps integrate this as well. Since this practice is about connecting with your body instead of your mind, check again for physical sensations related to your inner critic work.

4 When you feel tempted to set another weight loss goal, pause. Sit for a moment and do some deep belly breathing. Take stock of what's happening in your life. What is making you reduce your worth to what you weigh? Did someone say or do something to trigger you? Did you make a mistake, or underperform in some way? Did an old, upsetting memory surface? Are you going through a difficult transition? Are you bored? Life continues to provoke feelings like vulnerability, fear, anger, unworthiness, and lethargy. Instead of taking it out on your body, can you simply identify the feelings instead? Next, find someone to process with. A diet will not fix it, but feeling your life fully, finding support and getting to know yourself will.

_____

_____

_____

_____

_____

_____

_____

_____

_____

_____

_____

_____

_____

_____

_____

_____

_____

_____

_____

_____

_____

_____

_____

_____

_____

_____

_____

_____

_____

_____

_____

_____

_____

_____

_____

_____

_____

_____

_____

_____

_____

Chapter 4

PRACTICE TWO

GET HONEST

GET HONEST

Vulnerability sounds like truth and feels like courage. Truth and courage aren't always comfortable, but they are never weakness.

~Brené Brown

I'm walking down the center of Main Street, naked. Lining the route are people I've known throughout my life. They stare, point, and laugh. They're obviously embarrassed for me; wondering why I've chosen to walk unclothed through the middle of town. I wonder the same thing. I feel humiliated, scared, and alone; exposed in the most raw and demeaning way, with nowhere to hide.

This dream came during an especially intense time of craving and binging. My first thought upon waking was, "What can I eat today?", followed by a panicked fear of binging. Food was foremost in my mind all day, every day; nagging at me like a pounding headache. Every night brought a review of what I'd eaten, and judgment of myself as bad or good. I was paralyzed in a web of shame and isolation. Even my closest confidants were unaware of the depth of my suffering, and I had no idea how to share my pain.

Practice two brings an invitation to transparency and vulnerability. Allowing someone to see what we've done and who we've been can feel terrifying, but there is no movement toward peace without getting real.

Dr. Brené Brown, a research professor at the University of Houston Graduate College of Social

Work, studies vulnerability, courage, worthiness and shame. She says addiction and shame are hopelessly intertwined.

Addiction and shame go hand in hand. It is hard to understand where one starts and the other ends. Addiction leaves us feeling powerless, isolated, and unworthy. There is a strong sense of secrecy and silence about addiction. It is something that is easier to hide and just not talk about.

Shame and guilt are very different. Guilt means, "I *did* something bad." Shame means, "I *am* bad." Those of us struggling with food and our body feel deep shame about our behavior. Emotional eating is an isolating practice. The more you hide your eating, the more isolated you become; an incessant and destructive cycle.

I hid my binges, hoping no one would discover my shameful secret. What mattered most is I knew, and it was killing me. It was emotional blackmail, keeping me a prisoner to my fear of discovery. My secret held power only while it remained under wraps. Getting real is humbling, but brings enormous relief.

Our Practice Two Truth:

You will not heal your relationship with food and your body until you stop hiding your struggle.

Practice two is about getting honest; really, brutally honest. Not as in, "I sometimes eat too much when I'm not hungry," but telling your most shame-filled stories, in detail, to someone you trust.

"I dug food out of the trash last night," my friend confesses quietly, struggling to meet my gaze. She pauses, obviously bracing herself for a horrified reaction. "I thought throwing it out would help me stop binging, but nope. I went back,

dusted it off and devoured it." I nod emphatically and hug her, completely unfazed. I, too, have done this, and many clients have shared a similar story. My friend's eyes fill with tears, her relief palpable. She no longer feels alone.

Each time you talk about what it's really like when food has control, it loses a bit of its power. Maybe you've picked food out of the trash, purged by exercising or vomiting, or gone to great length and expense to buy, prepare, and binge on your favorite foods. At times, you may have switched your addiction to shopping, exercise or sex (More on this in Chapter 13). We hide, lie, and isolate with our lover...food. These behaviors do not mean you're a bad person; they mean you're a person in pain.

It's deeply empowering to reveal your stories. The open air of truth-telling acts as a healing balm to your wounded soul.

"I went to McDonalds in my pajamas last night, really late,"
my client whispers in a tearful voice. "I couldn't stop myself, I
wanted it so bad. I ate 3 Big Macs, a couple large orders of
fries, a shake, several pies, maybe more; I don't even remember.
I'm so scared. I can't fill myself up, I just can't. I got so sick
afterward. What do I do? I'm terrified someday I won't be
able to stop."

Feeling safe to share your secrets means finding
someone you trust implicitly; ideally someone with
a history of holding space for your really tough stuff.
If it's a friend or family member, it's respectful to give
them a heads up before you unload. For example,
"I'm learning to take better care of myself, and I need
to share some really tough stuff with someone. Are
you okay with being that person?" If it's a therapist
or wellness coach, you're paying them to listen and
keep things confidential, so dive right in.

Be aware of a desire to sugar coat your story to a

less gritty version. This is a messy path, and you must fully shed the dirt. Throw it all out there, and savor the relief of not carrying the heavy load on your own.

If you can't think of anyone you trust, start writing. Journaling is another powerful way to take the heaviness of your secrets and place them outside of yourself. Let the Universe, God, the Divine... whatever you call this supportive energy in your life...hold things for a while.

Another option is to find a support group. Overeater's Anonymous (OA) is a group based on the 12-step principles of Alcoholics Anonymous, but geared toward food compulsion and addiction. Many communities also have Meetup groups that provide support, encouragement, and a sense of belonging.

As you begin sharing your stories, other nagging

secrets may surface, seeking the air of truth. Many of my clients struggle with unaddressed relationship issues, increasing (or sometimes causing) their difficulty with food and their body. The discussion of healing relationships is beyond the scope of this book, but know this: If you are hiding from the truth about a relationship, your food dependence will be difficult (if not impossible) to heal. Why? Food helps to keep the story buried. The untold story nags at you (and you'll continue eating to stifle it) until you get honest and deal with the problem. Remember, it's a choice to continue living in pain, or learn to breathe deeply and freely again. I hope you courageously choose the latter.

INTEGRATE:

1 How does it feel to know you need to get vulnerable? Do you feel like throwing this book across the room? Sit in the feeling, and locate it in your body. Know that whatever you're feeling is normal and okay, even if it feels awful. The very essence of vulnerability is the discomfort it brings; that's why we avoid it! That discomfort is your growth point. Take a deep belly breath, find your courage and walk right into it.

2 Identify someone to be a sounding board for your stories of shame. Begin with one confession, and see how it feels. If your gut tells you this isn't the right person, step away and give it further thought. But, be mindful of your motivation. When you get to this point in the practice, it's easy to get scared and find fault, even with people who've earned your trust.

3 If no one comes to mind, start writing. Unleash it all on the page.

4 Since your recovery depends on ending isolation, check into support groups. Find your local Overeater's Anonymous chapter at *www.oa.org*. Search for Meetup Groups at *www.meetup.com*. Use search words like emotional eating, food addiction, or body image to find meetings in your area.

5 Fun activity: I urge you to watch Brené Brown's Ted Talk, *The Power of Vulnerability*. It's the third most-watched Ted Talk ever! She is witty, empowering and an amazing storyteller; and she'll motivate you to be fiercely honest and authentic. I also recommend any of her many books, found in all major online and brick-and-mortar bookstores. Check out *www.BreneBrown.com* for more information and some great free resources.

6 If you feel depressed (or even suicidal) as you share painful stories, *seek help immediately*. Call a family member, friend, or one of these helplines:

- *www.CrisisTextLine.org* lets you text message with one of their trained counselors.

- If you prefer to talk to a live person, call the National Suicide Prevention Lifeline 1-800-273-TALK (8255) for free and confidential support. Check out their website at *www.suicide preventionlifeline.org* for more information.

Remember...there is no shame in asking for help. On the contrary, it is a sign of amazing strength.

Get Honest

_____

_____

_____

_____

_____

_____

_____

_____

_____

_____

_____

_____

_____

Get Honest

_____

_____

_____

_____

_____

_____

_____

_____

_____

_____

_____

_____

_____

_____

Chapter 5

PRACTICE THREE

SIT WITH YOUR CRAVING

SIT WITH YOUR CRAVING

F*eel the pain that will end the pain. Don't drug it!*
~Dr. Christiane Northrup

I'm sitting on my couch, ready for a first attempt at this whole sitting-and-feeling thing. I'm dying to binge. A prickly, crawly sensation travels up my arms, itching from the inside out. My head feels like it's pulsating with heat and sweat. I'm scared; my muscles tensed and ready to help me bolt. Somehow, I manage to stay put and feel it all... the crawling skin, the fiery insides, the sweat. After a few minutes, I realize I'm okay. Whew. It was a miserable first experiment for sure, but I didn't die from the craving. Huh...

good to know! I jump up, head to the store, buy ice cream and have my binge. Thus begins my perfectly imperfect practice, Day One.

Apparently, I cried continually as a baby. My parents recall shoving bottles into my mouth throughout the night, desperate to quiet me. Mornings revealed a mess of empty bottles in and around the crib. I've always laughed along at this story, apologizing to them for being such a difficult baby.

Many of us learned very young to not cry or ache for anything. Don't let yourself feel empty; or even *feel* at all. If you do feel; for goodness sake, don't express it! Emptiness feels lonely, and emotions can be scary as hell. Food silently offers to fill the void. It also tamps down the emotions threatening to create discomfort for someone else.

Our Practice Three Truth:

Craving is your wise teacher, leading you to your unfinished work.

Some years ago, I wrote this letter:

Dear Craving,

You are completely ravenous and attention-seeking. I feel you as an underlying, inaccessible, insanity-making itch. You consume my thoughts and energy by day and at night you wake me with unquenchable hunger. I know I must sit here, feel the itchiness and wait for the root to show itself. I'm afraid. Caroline Myss says, "Habit is a hell to which people cling, in an attempt to stop the flow of change." Well, you're definitely my personal hell, and I'm exhausted. There's chocolate beckoning, but I'm overdue for a breakthrough. If I give in, I prolong my suffering. I commit to sitting here and waiting for your message. Please talk to me, and soon.

During the worst of times, no day went by without the miserable ache. All my thoughts centered on my next meal, often while seated at the current one. Every activity was planned around food.

Tibetan Buddhist nun and spiritual teacher Pema Chodron says if we continue *scratching the itch* of our craving, we block our healing. When that urge to eat hits like the worst itch you've ever felt, squirm and sweat but sit still, even if only for a few moments. Giving in makes misery your long-term companion. It seems counterintuitive to walk into the discomfort, but beneath it lies the real stuff you need to address. Feel the yearning, allowing emotions to step up, be validated and fully experienced. Anger, loneliness, shame, grief, fear, insecurity…As you embrace whatever surfaces, you experience a deep satiety food can *never* give.

Yes, this practice can be extremely uncomfortable.

But, distraction by compulsively eating creates *untold* discomfort, and keeps this unbearable cycle alive. Emotions remain buried, and cravings continue to trample your peace of mind.

In his book, *The Yoga of Eating,* Charles Eisenstein says to pause before eating to ask your body, "Do you really want this?" He next suggests locating the craving; finding the spot where it lives in your body, and sending your breath there for several moments before deciding to feed it. What might your body say when finally given a chance to weigh in?

The key, and this is crucially important: reassure yourself you have full permission to eat whatever you're craving after you practice, if you decide you still want to.

I'm sitting in a restaurant, watching my fellow diners casually order lavish, calorie-laden desserts. I've told myself I can't have any. My mouth waters at the thought of tiramisu or gelato. I close my eyes with a sigh, feeling deprived and alone. With a deep breath, my fledgling craving practice comes to mind... full permission, nothing off limits. I silently ask, "Ter, how do you feel? Are you still hungry? Do you really want dessert? Because, you can have anything you want. It's ok. No limits, remember?" Another deep breath. An unfamiliar but calming sense of complete satisfaction floods through me. My belly is full; I feel a bit nauseous at the thought of eating anything more. I can't believe it. I don't want dessert; not at all! Never before have I experienced this sense of freedom.

Sit with this idea: *Full Permission*. No rules, nothing off limits. As hard as it may be to believe, you'll be more willing and able to do healing work if you know your options are wide open. When there are no forbidden foods, you're faced with choices instead of limits. When you suddenly have permission to throw out the rules, you'll find yourself asking, "Do I even *want* to eat this?" Sometimes, we just want what we believe we can't have. Give yourself the power to decide.

A client experienced this ah-ha moment:

"Often what I'm swallowing down is a reaction or an interaction. I swallow my feelings and what I need to express. I can feel it physically in my gut when I do this. I also feel it physically when I speak my truth. My cravings are going away as I learn to speak up. I have less need to force things back down with food."

In my experience, there are two kinds of hunger signals. One overtakes the senses with an all-consuming, fiery persistence, demanding, *"Give me food, NOW."* The other nudges like a little child tugging on your sleeve. "Hey there," it says. "I could use something to eat when you get a chance." A loving response, without urgency or excess, brings quiet resolution. No fuss, no stress. You'll notice a comfortable familiarity to it, a "Hey...I know you!" feeling of warm recognition when you calmly respond to the sensation of real hunger.

When you're afraid to express yourself, this innate survival mechanism is interrupted. There's a frantic, urgent reaction to keep things tamped down with food. Feeding emotion is a losing battle, 100% of the time. When food is used as intended, there's a sweet surrender to life.

For years, fiery hunger burned through me, reducing me to a bingeing, overwrought, miserable mess. When fed with urgency and angst, it *always* wanted more. The food was ineffectual; it could never feed the real hunger within. Emotional hunger is like an overbearing parent, never satisfied with their child's efforts. You can be in agony with a too-full belly, but an incessant emptiness within insists you need more.

How can you distinguish between the two? Emotional hunger means a little bit of something isn't good enough; a bit of chocolate, or a dip of ice-cream. It means a desperate search for large amounts of something immediate, exciting and usually unhealthy.

With real, actual hunger, whatever is available suffices...even an apple or some vegetables. Feeding real hunger means nurturing your body so it can perform and function well.

When binging, you dodge life by looking outside yourself for a sense of aliveness. For someone else, it may be alcohol, sex, shopping, sports; it's all the same. Addiction is about numbing out, avoidance, and a desire for distraction from the unpredictable flow of life.

To heal your relationship with food, you must

acknowledge your desire to have things happen at your speed, in your timing. It means repeatedly returning to the worn, threadbare couch of surrender to the unknown. You may fear there is bad to be had by surrendering to the mystery, but within change lies the potential for joy, fulfillment and growth. Who doesn't want to experience that magical mystery tour? How can fear be greater than this potential super-sized combo of benefits? For emotional eaters, it is.

It's mid-morning, and I'm between client appointments. I'm hungry...honest-to-goodness, tummy-growling hungry. I've chosen to drink some water and wait for lunchtime. I'm very uncomfortable physically, but the psychological game haunts me most. I know I "can" eat since I'm hungry, so of course I want to grab the first opportunity to do so. Emotionally, I feel unsettled, nervous, jumpy. I've spent my life running from this feeling. Why? I cling to a thought running through my mind: "Just feel it, don't fill it." Most days, I brave any inconvenience to quell this sensation. The emptiness feels really scary. As I wait and breathe, my fear and anxiety slowly subside. I reassure myself I can eat soon, and that food is abundant. A little reassurance goes a long way. It's been an interesting exercise, and I feel empowered. In this moment, food did not win.

The hardest part about not eating immediately is the vacuum; just you and that gnawing sense of emptiness. Identifying, and eventually filling your real needs requires sitting in this void. It's a tough assignment.

Food brings only fleeting pleasure…a few minutes of appeasement deny a lifetime of unmet needs. So, here's your fork in the road…continue using food to fill the empty space, or stay with temporary discomfort and learn self-care. To finally do the latter and simply sit with unsettledness, itchiness and longing…this is the real work of the journey to peace.

Integrate:

1 Next time you're alone and craving (these two things often go together), pause for a moment.

2 Take several deep breaths into your belly.

3 Reassure yourself you can eat after this exercise, if you still want to.

4 Feel the craving, seeing if you can locate it in your body. If you can't, no worries. The important part of this exercise is to simply *feel* the craving instead of *thinking* about it.

5 Notice physical sensations, and feel them fully for as long as you can. See if you can identify traits of real hunger versus feeling hunger.

6 Notice any stories or emotions that arise.

7 When you're done, you're done; and now you decide if you still want to eat. No judgment, just a decision.

8 If you do eat, don't kick yourself; instead practice self-compassion. This is hard work you're doing!

9 Keep coming back to this practice: Breathe, give permission to eat after your practice, feel the craving, sit with it, locate it in your body, identify emotions, make a decision, practice compassion.

10 Write a letter to your craving. Let it know how you feel about it and what you need. Ask what it needs from you. Above all, remember even your craving is part of you, so express your

feelings respectfully. Your ultimate goal is self-love, remember? If you reject this part (or any part) of yourself, self-love and healing are impossible.

11 If emotions arise that feel like too much to handle alone, call someone you trust and talk it out. If your thoughts turn self-destructive, call or text one of the helplines listed at the end of Chapter 4. You are not alone.

Sit With Your Craving

_____

_____

_____

_____

_____

_____

_____

_____

_____

_____

_____

_____

_____

_____

_____

_____

_____

_____

_____

_____

_____

_____

_____

_____

_____

_____

_____

Sit With Your Craving

Chapter 6

PRACTICE FOUR

FEEL YOUR BINGES

FEEL YOUR BINGES

If something you eat makes you uncomfortable afterward, it's imperative to patiently feel and experience that discomfort. That way the experience of eating becomes integrated with all its effects, not just the initial mouth-pleasure.

~Charles Eisenstein, The Yoga of Eating

I've decided to stop eating sugar, and I miss it like someone else might miss an absent lover. Eating a sugary treat should be an innocuous indulgence, but for me it holds destructive power. Without fail, it throws me from equilibrium into compulsiveness and self-loathing. I find myself hunched over yet another bowl of ice cream, frustrated tears stinging my eyelids, promising myself I'll diet tomorrow, or do extra exercise for damage control. Food pretends to offer me everything, but it's an empty promise. Each time I succumb, I am betrayed and deeply wounded.

Even after doing this work for a while, binges may happen periodically. With continued practice, the intensity and frequency of binging decreases, and your awareness and growth increase. Whether you're just beginning, or have been on the journey for a while, the practice is the same.

Our Practice Four Truth:

You must feel the physical, emotional and mental effects of each binge as completely as you can.

I know this sounds crazy. Feeling the stuffed, gassy, headachy, depressed misery of a binge is the last thing we ever want to do. But, feeling these natural consequences is the only way to curtail future like-behavior. If you move to quickly detach from the resulting pain and discomfort, you won't feel it fully enough. Really experiencing a binge means eventually deciding you don't want to feel that way ever again.

Think for a moment about your overeating experiences, filled with both extremes of pleasure and pain. If you never experience the full spectrum, you'll only recall the initial pleasure and desirable sensations of the food's texture and taste. You must also feel the painful effects of binging to decide it's not worth it. It's our natural human instinct to avoid pain, but dodging discomfort keeps this destructive habit alive.

This practice is very similar to feeling your cravings. Literally sit down and feel the physical sensations of your bender: the pressure and discomfort in your belly, the headache, nausea, gas, bloating. Stay with it; breathe and feel.

Next, take stock of your emotional state. Are you itching to get relief through purging, exercise or a distraction of some sort? Are you beating yourself up for what you've chosen to do? Perhaps you're feeling hopeless, helpless, scared and alone. Feel it all, but don't act. Do give yourself some intense love and kindness. Imagine how you would support a cherished friend or loved one experiencing what you are, and offer the same to yourself.

So, now what? You've binged. You've taken time to feel the misery. The next step is forgiveness and moving on. It's done. I always yearned to undo my binges, and I tried through obsessive exercise or starting a new diet. The painful truth:

The only undoing is doing differently next time.

"Differently" may mean small steps, like bringing more awareness to the next binge. Eventually, it means a binge of reduced intensity, fewer binges, or perhaps none at all. This is a practice with moments of clarity, awareness, and healing; but also mistakes, losing ground, and do-overs. Take heart...you'll learn from all of it. Repeatedly feel it all, then love and forgive yourself. Feel, love and forgive.

A word on purging of any kind: it damages your body and spirit. Any means, whether over-exercising, vomiting, or use of laxatives harms you physically, emotionally, spiritually, and mentally. These practices do not allow you to heal. If you are unable to stop purging, please seek help right away. I *know* it's hard. I *know* it feels embarrassing and shameful, but strength lies in seeking help, not avoiding it. I did years of therapy to help me heal and consider this hard work my crowning achievement. It is truly the most loving thing you can do, and let us not forget the core of this healing process...*learning to fiercely love yourself*. Remember, this takes action. The shift from self-hatred to self-love is challenging. Being vulnerable enough to ask for help is the road home.

INTEGRATE:

1 After your next binge, sit down and feel everything.

2 First, note uncomfortable *physical* sensations. Name them out loud or in writing: *I feel bloated. My stomach feels like it's going to explode. I feel nauseous. I have a headache. I feel so fat.*

3 Next, observe your *emotions.* Identify the feelings and say or write them: *I feel scared. I feel ashamed. I feel so discouraged. I hate myself. I feel really alone.*

4 Talk to your confidante, support group, or a helpline about your post-binge feelings. Let some of the heaviness be held by others you trust.

5 Practice using forgiving, loving language as you journal, talk about your experiences, and in your self-talk. Remember...fierce, protective self-love is your home base.

6 If you purge through vomiting or laxatives, seek professional help right away. You must address this destructive habit before you can fully heal.

7 Repeat the above steps as needed. Over time, fully experiencing the pain of binging helps you decide it's not worth it.

Feel Your Binges

_____

_____

_____

_____

_____

_____

_____

_____

_____

_____

_____

_____

_____

_____

_____

_____

_____

_____

_____

_____

_____

_____

_____

_____

_____

_____

_____

_____

_____

_____

_____

Feel Your Binges

_____

_____

_____

_____

_____

_____

_____

_____

_____

_____

_____

_____

_____

Chapter 7

PRACTICE FIVE

DEAL WITH YOUR SHADOW

DEAL WITH YOUR SHADOW

T*he person we choose to be automatically creates a dark double — the person we choose not to be.*

~*Thomas Moore*

My shadow is showing itself in the cringe-worthy behavior of others. The more I recoil from someone else's actions or attitudes, the more likely it's present in me. This is a painful realization. Today I heard several women gossiping about a "friend." I felt sick and disgusted; even more so when I remembered my shadow practice. This gossip trait I abhor must exist within me! When I stop judging others, I will stop judging myself. If I don't, the food craziness and body hatred will continue, and the very thought makes me wearier than I can ever describe.

In Jungian psychology, the shadow is part of your unconscious mind, consisting of traits you've repressed. It's usually the stuff you are terrified others will discover about you. Your shadow keeps you from being fully genuine, experiencing real intimacy with others and finding healing on this food and body journey.

Your shadow reveals agonizing qualities you've avoided at all costs. When I began my own shadow work, I had to confront jealousy, insecurity, control, insensitivity, and fear; just to name a few. To take a good look in this dimly lit, grimy mirror reflecting back to you the worst of yourself is no picnic. It is, however, a healing step that cannot be skipped; not if you truly want to end your struggle with food and your body.

Our Practice Five Truth:

Until you confront and heal your shadow, you will continue using food to bury traits you believe are undesirable.

Confronting the shadow means you have to actually do something about what you unearth. Ignoring what you find blocks your healing. Descent into the shadow can feel dangerous, but Jung offers these reassuring words: "Every descent is followed by an ascent." In other words, be brave and face it, and the shadow will finally cease pulling your strings like an invisible puppet master.

You're probably familiar with this experience: you don't *want* to eat; you don't *need* to eat; you feel desperate *not* to eat, but you do it anyway. These moments hold valuable clues about what you're denying or hiding from. Instead of using food to subdue whatever wants to claw its way to the light, pause to sit, breathe, and get curious. "Why am I eating right now? What is this urgent longing really about? What am I pushing down, or away? What don't I want to face? What am I afraid of?"

The biggest gift of embracing your shadow side comes from understanding yourself more fully. Your relationship with food, your body and other people changes as you discover the things you've been denying. You'll feel more freedom to be yourself, stop hiding, and freely express what you need to say.

How do you get started on shadow work? In his book, *Yoga and the Quest for the True Self*, Stephen Cope says, "Our shadow is anything we're sure we are not." The painful truth: Whatever you detest in others is present within. Look at what you gossip about, criticize, and abhor in others, and make a list. These are denied parts of yourself mirrored back to you. Gossip is a common way of shadow-dodging. It's easy to see the faults of others, but so difficult to look at our own stuff. Gary Zukav says it beautifully in *Soul to Soul: Communications from the Heart*:

When you have an emotional reaction to what you see, you are judging. That is your signal that you have an issue inside of yourself - with yourself - not with the other person. If you react to evil, look inside yourself for the very thing that so agitates you, and you will find it. If it were not there, you will simply discern, act appropriately, and move on.

This is where the hard work and transformation begins, so buckle up! Part of healing the shadow is facing down the strong resistance you'll inevitably feel to what you find. It takes incredible courage to shine a light on and own the undesirable traits you discover. Enter your practice of fierce self-love and forgiveness. You are, after all, a human being taking on the daunting task of learning about and becoming a better version of yourself. This can't happen if you never confront your darkness.

Shadow discovery continues lifelong, but with time becomes more fulfilling than painful. You greatly enhance your food and body practice as you continue welcoming and loving all parts of yourself, shadow included.

Carl Jung also says, "Whatever is wrong in the world is in himself, and if he only learns to deal with his own shadow, he has done something real for the world." A more real and conscious *You* is not only a gift to the world, but a required practice on this healing path.

INTEGRATE:

1 Think about or journal: What traits in other people drive me crazy? Make a list. Notice your reaction, especially any resistance to the idea these traits exist in you. For now, you don't have to do anything but bring awareness to the practice and sit with the feelings that arise.

2 Begin a practice of ownership. Using the list you made in #1, ask to be shown specific examples of these traits at work in your life. Write down examples that come to mind. Sit with any discomfort at seeing yourself in this light. Apply liberal amounts of patience, kindness and grace.

3 When you catch yourself acting out your shadow, express gratitude for being shown where healing is needed. Be sure to welcome these newly discovered, cast-off parts of you. Consider how you might act

differently in these areas. Where your tendency is to condemn and hate what's revealed, apply love, acceptance, and forgiveness instead. Stay open to the healing power of this shadow work.

4 This practice continues life-long, but with time becomes less painful and more fulfilling. You notice cross over into your food and body practice as you continue welcoming and loving all parts of yourself, including your shadow.

Chapter 8

Practice Six

Find Moderation and Balance

FIND MODERATION AND BALANCE

Abstinence is a path of choosing between profound suffering or abject failure. Moderation is a more humane choice. Balance brings more fulfillment and less suffering.

~Earon Davis

I lived by extreme and restrictive food rules for many years. I've been gluten free, sugar-free, and vegetarian. I did a chicken and fish, but no red meat phase. I went grain free, low-glycemic, and low histamine. I even (to my husband's dismay) combined them all for a while. One eye-opening day, I realized my life had become one very long list of everything I told myself I couldn't or shouldn't have. I decided I'd had enough of the craziness, and quite literally changed my eating attitude that day.

My new approach? Eat what sounds good, but make mostly healthy choices. Most importantly, listen to (and feel) the effects of these choices on my body, rather than to some arbitrary plan based on what someone else discovered they need.

Our Practice Six Truth:

Seeking balance and moderation by listening to your body's unique needs leads to improved health, increased vitality, weight normalization and a halt to food obsession and worry.

An in-depth discussion of nutrition is beyond the

scope and intention of this book. There are plenty of excellent resources on nutrition already available. Obviously, there are certain foods that help everyone thrive, but my intention is helping you to notice what makes *your* body happy. The eating plan that makes sense and works for the long term is the one honoring what your body wants. Contained within you is all the information you need to eat well, enjoy good health and feel great.

It's important to distinguish between messages from your body and those of your mind. The mind will *always* say yes to french fries or ice cream, but the body...not so much. Don't let your mind do the meal planning!

As you develop a healthier lifestyle, please do consider current research and dietary recommendations; just don't forget to personalize your plan based on what makes *your* body thrive. To get the wheels turning for you, here's what I discovered from listening to *my* body over time:

- I feel best if my diet includes a lot of vegetables, a little fruit, and just a few grains. I need some meat to feel grounded and healthy. Chicken and fish make me feel best, but about once or twice a month I need a moderate amount of red meat to keep me feeling grounded and calm.

- Processed sugar remains my forbidden love. It takes very little to give me a rash, headache, and suppressed immunity. It also gifts me with a restless spirit and an urge to binge. When I indulge, it is in small amounts. Even natural sugars like maple syrup, honey, coconut sugar, and agave can create problems when I use them in excess. I use a bit of natural stevia when I really want something sweet. Research on other sweeteners like xylitol and sugar alcohols gives me pause; enough so that I don't use them. Do your own research, but remember: it's possible to trigger cravings and a desire to binge on *anything*, including things touted as sugar free and *healthy*. (See helpful research resources at the end of the chapter.)

• My central nervous system can't manage caffeine. It makes me a nervous, jittery, sleepless mess.

• More than an occasional glass of wine also robs my sleep, tanks my immunity and gives me a headache.

• Probably my most important discovery, and the one that benefits everyone, without exception: I use my body's built-in portion control sensor… hunger. I eat when I'm truly, physically hungry, and stop when I'm full. Not bursting at the seams full, but satiated. Discerning this difference takes some practice, but is well worth the patience and effort required.

Please keep in mind: Everyone's body has different needs. The lifestyle I describe above works well for *me*, but this doesn't mean it's the best approach for you. While it's perfectly appropriate to see how you respond to caffeine, sugar, alcohol and various protein sources, resist the temptation to use my example as an exact template for your body's journey. You get to discover your unique blueprint… how exciting! Do brace yourself, however; you may get a message you'd rather not hear. I still sometimes grieve the things I can no longer tolerate, but the sacrifice is worth the benefit of living in a healthy, centered, stable body.

It's important to notice not only what you *can't* have, but also everything you can! After I identified what doesn't jive with my body, I turned my focus to gratitude for and enjoyment of everything that makes me feel great. After a while, that good feeling overpowers the craving for stuff that doesn't work for you.

It's also important to be aware of moderation's tendency to be tricky; easily manipulated by a creative, craving mind. In the past, I've found myself *moderately binging* on a wide-variety of foods; fooling myself that, because I wasn't eating very much of any one thing, it didn't count as binging. This invariably led to obsession, craving and no peace of mind to be found.

Another trick your mind might play: telling you it's okay to overeat on healthy food. One evening about a year ago, I'd fixed myself a beautiful dinner...steamed kale and curried lentils, avocado smoothed on a rice cake and homemade tabbouleh with fresh peas and cucumber. A crisp green apple waited in the wings for dessert. It was too much food, and about halfway through, I was already getting full. Anxiety started to build, and I found myself eating more quickly, hoping to fool my body into accepting more than it needed. I finished my meal with an excessively full belly and a deep sense of dissatisfaction.

My desperation to continue the pleasurable experience of eating meant I wasn't listening. I didn't need more food, healthy or not. I needed some deep breaths and to simply *be* with myself for a few moments. It's the same practice, renewed each time...pause, notice the craving, wait for the message, try to choose wisely. On this particular night, I quickly identified the real cause of my emptiness. My husband was traveling for work and I was hibernating at home, feeling lonely. Instead of taking steps to connect with others, I was using food as my friend; a role it can never fill.

Some years ago, feeling addicted and out of control, I took one of many breaks from sugar. About a week in, I had a painful epiphany: I had been avoiding favorites like ice cream and chocolate, but making (and consuming) copious amounts of very sweet granola. I was missing the point and sabotaging myself, in a big way. My dependency on sugar was alive and well, being fed by something *healthy*. I was clinging to what felt safe and familiar: asking food to impart life's sweetness. I had to reassure my vulnerable self that sweetness is widely available; I just needed to look past my plate.

If you're thinking this practice sounds like a lot of work, you're right. Rest assured that the payoff for listening to your body and feeding it accordingly is truly abundant. Instead of feeling lethargic, overstuffed and depressed, you get to savor life as the energetic, vibrantly healthy and happy version of yourself you're meant to be.

Remember...every relationship takes time to develop. Be patient and loving with your body as it learns to trust you again.

INTEGRATE:

1 The next time you have an urge to overeat, pause. Breathe. *Really listen* for what's behind the craving. For instance, I know I crave sweetness every day, but the ease, convenience, and instant gratification of sugar is not the answer. It is an answer, but not the sweetness I truly seek. List what you discover.

2 Notice how you feel physically after eating or drinking anything. I highly recommend keeping a food diary, listing the time you ate, your specific intake and how your body feels. Don't get too crazy about details; just jot down some descriptive words like fuzzy brain, gassy, nauseous, lethargic. I also pay attention to the state of my mind after eating or drinking. Do I feel unsettled? Depressed? Angry with myself? You're finding connections between your food intake and your physical and mental health.

3 Start an intentional gratitude practice. Notice the abundance you're able to enjoy! Intentionally giving thanks (in whatever way is meaningful for you) creates a powerful, positive shift.

4 Look for your shadow. What are you avoiding by adopting strict rules around food? One hint: look for a need for control, which can simply be a desire to feel safe. What's happening that makes you feel a need for extra safety and predictability? Where do you feel vulnerable? Fearful? Uncertain?

5 Open a conversation with yourself, which may feel silly at first. Perhaps you need self-nurture, play, or some stillness? Ask! Over time, you'll get answers and be able to offer yourself more of what you really need. As answers come, record them in your journal.

6 As always, listen to your hunger; your body only needs so much food. Notice any resistance

to that satiated feeling. Sit with it and ask again: What do I *really* yearn for?

7 Online resources I find invaluable:

• Dr. John Douillard (www.LifeSpa.com)

• Dr. Christiane Northrup (www.DrNorthrup.com)

• Dr. Joseph Mercola (www.Mercola.com)

_____

_____

_____

_____

_____

_____

_____

_____

_____

_____

_____

_____

_____

Chapter 9

PRACTICE SEVEN

LEARN TO PLAY

LEARN TO PLAY

What most people don't realize is it's not the work part of exercise they hate, it's the boredom!
~*Jonathan Fields*

Without movement, the body cannot thrive or survive. We are truly artwork in action! Our bones, muscles, joints, connective tissue, blood, organs, lymph system; every part is created to benefit from physical activity. It's impossible to stay mentally, physically and emotionally healthy and viable for the long term without moving the masterpiece that is your body on a regular basis.

In a recent Time magazine article, *The New Science of Exercise*, genetic metabolic neurologist Dr. Mark Tarnopolsky raves, "If there were a drug that could do for human health everything that exercise can, it would likely be the most valuable pharmaceutical ever developed." He goes on to stress that the scientific benefits of exercise, like slower aging, improved mood, reduction in chronic pain and better vision are real, measurable and almost immediate.

Sadly, for most of us exercise means dread and obligation. Perhaps you've experienced this: you know you should exercise, but you really, really don't want to. You manage to drag yourself to your workout, counting the minutes until it's over. Or, maybe exercise has become an obsessive attempt to control and fix your body. Neither approach is a great way to make this essential practice a life-giving habit. Since staying active is our natural state of being, why is it so hard to get going?

The problem is, rather than finding joy in playing and moving, physical fitness has become about damage control. If you bargain with your body, agreeing to love it *after* it achieves a laundry list of changes, exercise always feels like drudgery. Nobody gets motivated by a harsh critique. Enter your self-love practice. When you accept yourself, perceived faults and all, your attitude about exercise begins to shift.

Also, it's important to remember there's a brilliantly crafted, well-funded and dishonest marketing machine working against you; whose survival depends on you remaining dissatisfied with your appearance. Its job is to fabricate the unrealistic body expectations that haunt women everywhere.

Our Practice Seven Truth:

When you stop using exercise as a flaw-fixer, you'll feel free to simply move, play and have fun without rules.

Let's get the numbers and statistics out of the way. Current recommendations from the World Health Organization and U.S. Centers for Disease Control and Prevention are to accumulate 150 minutes of moderate-intensity aerobic exercise a week. Average it out over a week, and it's only about 22 minutes a day! Not so overwhelming, right? Twice-weekly strength training is also part of the official recommendation, but any activity that strengthens your muscles counts. Think vigorous yard or house work, gardening, shoveling snow, climbing on a jungle gym or a rock wall with your kids; any activity that gets you lifting, pushing, pulling, and squatting. You don't have to go to a weight room, although that's fine too, if you enjoy it.

Intermittent exercise (adding up small amounts of movement throughout your day) is a highly-underrated way to accumulate your minutes. I recently experienced the benefits of this approach while stuck at my desk for an 8-week health coaching contract. I had to get creative about staying active so I made it a game, challenging myself to get moving in the few minutes between calls. Sometimes I did some squats or lunges. Other days I focused on pushups or timed planks, or threw in some yoga. On my lunch break and at the end of the day, I took a 10-15-minute walk. Not only did I accrue enough activity to really benefit my health, I felt energetic throughout my day.

The shift to thinking of exercise as *play* rather than *work* looks different for everyone. For me, play means hiking, yoga and walks with my hubby. I also can't wait to put on some great music and hop on my spinning bike. For you, maybe it's a bike ride outdoors, heading to the playground with your kids, skiing, or playing a sport. Recently, my sister was surprised to discover she loves to play golf. What you do doesn't matter, as long as you move your body in a way that raises your heart rate, challenges your muscles, makes you smile, and feels great; before, during, and after.

Keep in mind...fitness is a multibillion dollar industry. While there are well-intentioned people selling exercise programs, too often someone found what worked for them and decided it was the answer for everyone (and a great way to make money). Don't believe anyone claiming there's only one way to be fit and healthy. It may be a great approach, but it's just *one* way. Find what you love. You don't have to spend a ton of money, or maybe any at all. Just move!

Remember my story from Chapter 3, when my excitement to reach the playground made my heart leap with anticipation? It's fun to try recapturing that feeling as an adult!

INTEGRATE:

1 Pick a day this week to go outside and walk, run, skip, jump, hike, head to the playground; whatever sounds appealing. If the weather doesn't cooperate, turn on some music and dance in your living room!

2 Another great option: the various 7-Minute Workout apps you can download for your phone. Most are free! You get a full-body heart-pumping and muscle strengthening workout in 7 minutes. Repeat three times, and you've met your daily quota of aerobic exercise and strength training!

3 If you're just starting out, don't worry about time for now; just notice how it feels to move without rules or restrictions. Feel your muscles flexing, joints bending, lungs expanding and heart beating faster. Notice if there's discomfort

anywhere, and breathe into that place. Bonus points: take someone along, and laugh as you play. (**Note:** *Pain is another matter. Any sharp sensation means stop and adjust and, if it continues, stop altogether and get a second opinion.*)

4 The next time you have a highly-scheduled day, make a plan. See where you can inject some movement. If you work in an office, get up every 30-60 minutes and take a walk, even if it's just up and down the hall or stairs. If you have a private office, try some squats, lunges, or push-ups (against the wall or on your knees are effective, too!). Skip the elevator in favor of stairs, and park as far away as you reasonably (and safely) can. Set aside part of your lunch break to move in some way. Every bit counts!

5 While it can be fun to keep track of your progress via use of an iPhone app, Fitbit, or

other fitness tracker, the tendency to begin focusing on numbers (calories expended, exercise minutes, etc.); rather than how your body *feels* is destructive to your new, healthier focus. Remember: you're shifting away from body-fixing and toward fun and play. The temptation is real; don't let it ensnare you again.

6 Grab your journal and record what you notice during and after your chosen exercise session. Note physical sensations, emotions, thoughts. Get to know how your body wants to move, while being respectful of the fact that this will change depending on what's happening in your life on a given day. For example, pushing your body to play hard when it's asking for mindful, calm movement goes against the innate body wisdom you're trying to access for making meaningful, lasting change.

7 For some of the latest exercise research, summarized in body-friendly, interesting

language, check out the rest of the Time Magazine article quoted earlier in the chapter, *The New Science of Exercise*, at *http://time.com/4475628/the-new-science-of-exercise*

Chapter 10

PRACTICE EIGHT

MOTHER YOURSELF

MOTHER YOURSELF

---

*I used to spend so much time reacting and responding to
everyone else that my life had no direction. Other people's
lives, problems, and wants set the course for my life. Once I
realized it was okay for me to think about and identify what
I wanted, remarkable things began to take place in my life.*
~Melody Beattie

Some years ago, I had a client who catered
exclusively to the needs of her family, church,
and employer. Exhaustion and an uncomfortably
overweight body were her reward. Her dreams,
creativity, and soul's purpose were lost in the

destructive tidal wave of other-care known as codependency. The extra weight on her body remained stubbornly fixed, because she couldn't shed the weight of carrying the world and other people on her shoulders.

My client was confused and extremely frustrated about this inability to lose weight. As we took an honest look at her life, the issues became clear. She felt guilty about asking her husband and children to take on extra responsibility at home. She feared they might not do it *right*. Every night after the chaos of dinner, dishes, homework, baths, crises, and tuck-ins was finally over, she collapsed in a chair, nursing a big bag of chips as her reward. The luxury and pleasure of eating made her feel special; finally, a tiny part of the day was about her. She longed to be a priority sometimes; to feel special and have her own interests and pursuits. She is, after all, not just a mother, wife and employee.

She's also a person in her own right, desperately needing the soothing balm of self-attention.

This is an all too common tale I hear in my coaching sessions. Women are raised to be caretakers, charged with satisfying everyone around them. When we have young children and grandchildren, the expectations and demands increase. Despite being exhausting, and devastating to our health and wellness, there is admittedly a sense of identity born from being the savior of our world.

In the meantime, my client continued reporting to her coaching sessions feeling overweight, overwhelmed, exhausted and extremely unhappy. She was also angry as hell, but unwilling and unable to say so.

Our Practice Eight Truth:

You cannot give well when your well is empty.

Codependency means putting the needs of other people before your own, *to your detriment*. For those of us on the food and body journey, it perpetuates the struggle and prevents healing. Your body and spirit are asking for attention, right now. For a while, you'll get a gentle nudge, asking you to make changes. Eventually, the prodding becomes forceful, with a painful wakeup call of extra weight, illness, injury, or depression; sometimes all of the above. The key is not waiting to make adjustments until this happens.

It truly is important to be helpful and loving to others, and sometimes the needs of your family, work, school, or church need to come first. When it becomes a problem is when it's happening so often that it affects *your* health and well-being. You're a more effective ambassador of love and care to those around you when you offer the same to yourself. We do everyone a disservice when we give from a place of emptiness. We've all been there...making dinner, or driving the kids to soccer practice and feeling tired and resentful; wanting to be anywhere but present in that moment - with the people we cherish. This is not helpful or truly loving to anyone, yourself included. Finding a balance benefits everyone; but most importantly, you.

INTEGRATE:

1 Arrange for some time to yourself, even half an hour. Sit down with a pen and paper. Close your eyes and take some breaths deep into your belly. Picture the things you do for others. Take an honest inventory. Now, pick one thing someone else can take on. It might be asking your husband or partner to be in charge of dinner one night a week, or showing your kids how to fold their own laundry. As you identify possibilities, notice the feelings arising... guilt, control (They won't do it right), fear (What if they don't need me anymore?). Breathe, relax, feel. Allow it all to be there. Open your eyes and write your experience...feelings, concerns, sabotaging thoughts (why it won't work). Spill it all, and let the pages hold it for you; just for now.

2 Decide if you want to act. If you just can't do it yet, okay. Promise to revisit the possibility on a

daily basis until you're ready. Remember, a crucial trait you need on this journey is courage. Change isn't easy, but if you truly want to make progress, it's time to dip your toes into the change pool. Start with something small. It's also good to let your husband, partner, or another trusted person know what you're working on.

3 Notice how it feels when you do something for someone else. Do you feel happy and fulfilled, or resentful and drained? Where do the feelings live in your body? Listen for signs of imbalance. Remember, it's wonderful to give of yourself and your time to others. It becomes a problem when it negatively affects you and your health.

_____

_____

_____

_____

_____

_____

_____

_____

_____

_____

_____

_____

_____

_____

Chapter 11

PRACTICE NINE

LEARN TO BE STILL

LEARN TO BE STILL

*I*t's just another day in paradise, as you stumble to your bed. You'd give anything to silence those voices ringing in your head. You thought you could find happiness just over that green hill. You thought you would be satisfied, but you never will. Learn to be still.

~Don Henley and Stanley Lynch

I attended my first yoga class 14 years ago. It was decidedly *not* love at first down dog. I was in the midst of a fitness career, teaching and training clients in weightlifting, kickboxing, spinning and boot camp classes. Yoga asked me to slow down and be present in my body, but I had spent my life running *away* from it. And, the meditation piece of yoga? Forget it. Sitting quietly and doing nothing made no sense to me. It meant I had to face my active mind and feel stuff I didn't want to feel, and I was having none of it.

After 3 years of fighting and resisting, I finally relented to the quiet voice within, telling me to practice yoga. Even after completing yoga teacher training in 2013, meditation remained my nemesis. I really despised it, constantly battling my relentlessly jabbering mind. I convinced myself that *my* yoga practice didn't need to include meditation. It just wasn't for me, I assured myself, in spite of an inner voice gently inviting me to take a seat.

It took me a full year of teaching yoga before I surrendered to meditation. Every time I asked for life guidance, the answer was the same: *Be still.*

This guidance came at a tough time. A cross-country move, after living in the Midwest for 28 years, had pushed me into a deep depression. I felt lost…no job, no friends, an empty nest. Our dog died a few months after the move, and several family members developed serious health problems. No obvious answers or relief presented. Divine wisdom speaks quietly and patiently for a while, but it does have limits. It knows what we need, and does what it takes to get us there. I finally collapsed into meditation out of sheer exhaustion and lack of options. I started with a few minutes…setting a timer and sweating my way through every second. Admittedly, this was no centered, Zen experience in the beginning. It was torture being alone with myself and my thoughts.

Eventually, my surrender to stillness brought huge relief. I kept at it, gradually increasing to ten minutes, sometimes even 20. Unbelievably, I started to crave it. I noticed an unfamiliar stillness within me, and a deep sense of love and connection for myself and those around me. I felt less rushed, without a constant need to seek something I couldn't even name. I was better able to sit with my emotions, cravings, and questions. I realized I was being asked to trust, wait, and accept life as it came.

Our Practice Nine Truth:

Everything ceases to make sense, especially your relationship with your body and food, if you don't take time to be still and present with yourself.

I understand how scary it is to sit in silence, having lived with the same fear for such a long time. I still resist stillness on many days! Like everything on this journey, the key is making this practice uniquely yours.

For me, being still involves yoga and meditation.

For you, perhaps it's a quiet, mindful walk in nature, or sitting on your deck or porch with a cup of tea and some deep, intentional breaths. Choose your own way to unplug from outside stimulation, and tune into yourself.

Emotional eating and body hatred are kept alive by distraction and disconnection; by maintaining a frenzied, fast-paced existence. To break this cycle, you must find your calm, connected center. It is here you learn to approach your food and body practice with love, devotion and awareness.

A favorite quote of mine, source unknown: "Prayer is when you talk to God (Divine, Universe, Source… insert your term here), and meditation is when you stop to hear the response." Wisdom and a sense of peace are available when you hit pause on your life and simply listen.

INTEGRATE:

1 Forget everything you've read or heard about the "right" way to be still. You don't need to call it meditation if that word is too loaded or intimidating for you.

2 Set a timer for what may seem a ridiculously manageable amount of time, even just a few minutes.

3 Put away your phone, iPad, and computer. Turn off the TV, music, or radio.

4 Find a relatively quiet, calming, restful spot. Sit in a chair or on the floor, or even lay down if that feels best (and if you can stay awake!). Get comfy with a nice, straight spine. If you're walking, do your best to get in nature and away from concrete and people.

5 Take deep, intentional belly breaths. If you're not walking, it's helpful to close your eyes.

6 Notice as thoughts and images arise, but without judging them or yourself. If upsetting thoughts are nagging at you, reassure yourself you can revisit them later. Just keep coming back to your breath, over and over...inhale, exhale.

7 When the time is up, commend yourself for practicing self-care and get on with your day.

8 Repeat daily when possible, with no expectations for extending the time until you're ready.

9 If you miss a day, just resume when you can. Keep in mind that a regular routine of stillness will make it easier to maintain and see the benefits of your practice.

10 Great resources:

• Meditation Secrets for Women; Discovering Your Passion, Pleasure and Inner Peace, by Camille Maurine and Lorin Roche, Ph.D., is a wonderful book about making stillness a personalized practice.

• Oprah Winfrey and Deepak Chopra's 21-day Meditation Experience, available free online at www.chopracentermeditation.com. The meditations are gently guided with an introduction and some lovely, soothing music throughout. It makes getting started a bit less lonely and overwhelming.

• Christiane Northrup is a board-certified OB/GYN physician and leading authority in the field of women's health. Her website, www.drnorthrup.com, is an invaluable source of information, including several wonderful blogs on the benefits of meditation.

• Dr. John Douillard, based in Boulder, Colorado, is a globally-recognized expert in natural health, Ayurveda and sports medicine. His website, www. Lifespa.com, offers helpful information on many health and wellness topics, including the benefits of meditation and stillness. He also offers a guided meditation course.

_____

_____

_____

_____

_____

_____

_____

_____

_____

_____

_____

_____

_____

_____

Learn to Be Still

_____

_____

_____

_____

_____

_____

_____

_____

_____

_____

_____

_____

Learn to Be Still

_____

_____

_____

_____

_____

_____

_____

_____

_____

_____

_____

_____

_____

Chapter 12

PRACTICE TEN

DITCH THE SCALE,
MAGAZINES AND MIRRORS

DITCH THE SCALE,
MAGAZINES AND MIRRORS

The mind is always asking you to do something you have already done so many times before. Every time, you see that by doing it, nothing is achieved. What else can madness be?

~Osho

The Scale

It's Saturday morning, and time for my favorite weekend tradition of breakfast with friends. First, there's a test to pass. I head to the bathroom, lock the door, and pull out the scale. Not wanting to risk any extra weight, I discard my pajamas. I step lightly and gingerly onto the scale, hoping this additional tactic will help my cause. This moment determines if there's a pastry in my near future.

Shit. No cinnamon roll for me. I'm up 2 pounds from yesterday. Suddenly, my body feels huge, where moments ago it felt fine. As I dress, my clothes feel tightly bound to my body, as if they're constricting my breath and movement. I glower at my reflection, seeing an enormous body reflected back, although I'm actually at a healthy weight. My connection to reality and all joy and anticipation about my day has evaporated, all because I believe I'm defined by a number.

Magazines

A huge sigh escapes me; my eyes clamped shut in frustration. I've been exercising and dieting relentlessly for years, still hoping to carve out the body of steel I see in magazines, like the one lying in a crumpled heap beside my chair. This latest edition beckoned from the grocery checkout, promising a new and magical combination of exercises. I believed the lies again, gazing in wonder at the fitness model with firm thighs and a tiny, toned butt. No matter that she is 6 inches taller than the average woman, or that she's been airbrushed and digitally enhanced into a caricature of herself. I can't see past my fervent belief I am nothing without that body. I feel betrayed and disillusioned, and teeter on the brink of my next binge.

Mirrors

I stride purposefully down the sidewalk, feeling good about life, and even my body. Out of habit, I glance sideways at my reflection in a shop window.

Not liking what I see, I slow my pace at the next storefront. Like air leaving an escaped balloon, my self-esteem splutters and fizzles to the sidewalk. My thoughts begin their familiar, torturous abuse.

Seriously? You thought you looked good in these jeans? UGH. You look dumpy and disgusting. You idiot...why didn't you wear higher heels to make your legs look longer? You definitely need to do more squats and lunges. Oh, and add the butt machine. Too bad about those shin splints...today you run extra mileage anyway. How can you live with yourself?

No longer do I feel good...about anything. Another peaceful, purposeful day is squandered because of my need for reflection-reassurance.

These stories represent a small fraction of the painful weigh-ins, reflection checks, and magazine betrayals I experienced over many years. The insanity created by these self-esteem measuring tools is nothing compared to the insanity of continuing to pursue them. Why return to false means of measuring our worth, when the result is always misery? Let's get honest...have you ever felt uplifted and good about yourself after reading a beauty or fitness magazine? It's self-abuse, and I encourage you to seriously consider halting these habits.

Many years have passed since I weighed myself on a regular basis. I no longer own a scale; I get weighed at my yearly doctor's appointment. I wouldn't dream of reading a fashion or fitness magazine. Other than when I get ready in the morning, I avoid looking at my reflection in mirrors or shop windows. I know what I look like, so why keep checking? It's a maddening habit at best, and an incredibly self-destructive one at worst. It keeps the myth alive...that our worth is measured by collecting appearance points.

Our Practice Ten Truth:

Obsessive weigh-ins, reflection checks and reading beauty and fitness magazines prevent self-acceptance, and perpetuate unhealthy food behavior, body hatred, and distorted thinking.

Please read and consider this Truth repeatedly. It may take some time before you believe it. We're brainwashed to believe fabricated rules about what's acceptable and beautiful in the female form. These measures are set by someone else deciding what you should weigh, wear, and do. It's time to create and live your own set of standards.

It's not easy; the media and Madison Avenue are convincing in their limited view of beauty. It's hard to see through their murky message to find your own sense of beauty and power. Tune them out, and yourself back in.

For me, feeling worthwhile and beautiful comes from:

- *Doing what I love, and pursuing my passions.*
- *Taking good care of my body because I want to feel good, not because I'm flawed and must be fixed or look different.*
- *Finding a fun way to exercise.*
- *Having an intentional practice of self-love that includes a fierce sense of protectiveness for myself and my body.*

When I finally stopped denigrating myself, I could feel my body trust me again. Blaming your body for your discomfort and distress is really unfair. It does its best every day based on what you offer...the types of food and activity, stress reduction, rest. It trusts you to take care of it and, when you don't, it can only respond in kind. It doesn't have a choice.

So, to get angry with your body when it puts on weight or gets sick is a backward response. When I grasped how completely vulnerable my body is to my actions, it completely changed my perspective and relationship to it.

When you look outside yourself for validation and self-esteem (the scale, media, a mirror), it's impossible to connect with what you really need. Remember: this journey is about tuning *out* the noise, turning *inward* to listen, and responding in kind.

The next time you feel like you've gained a little weight, before taking any corrective action like going on a diet, purging or increasing your exercise, stop. Sit and belly breathe for a moment or two. Identify what makes you feel heavier...tighter pants, perhaps? Knees hurting again? Brain fog from sugar? An overall sense of unsettledness? Whatever it is, just notice and feel. Write it all down.

Now, without judgment, inventory how you've been treating your body lately...what you've been eating, how much you're moving, how much rest you're getting, the amount of water you're drinking. If your inventory reveals you're not taking good care of yourself, *that's* useful information to work with.

Knowing the number on the scale is often *not* helpful. Recall for a moment what it feels like to see that needle inching upward. It sucks all the joy out of life and takes away any motivation for healthy behavior change. Chances are, you'll feel like heading for the kitchen, saying *screw it* all the way. Listening to your body's feedback can feel frustrating initially, but it's nothing compared to the silent scolding from the scale.

Give yourself a break, and stop willingly abusing yourself with external self-esteem measures. Trust *yourself* instead. Become a partner with your body, and watch a beautiful, helpful and very useful relationship unfold.

Note: If your physician has told you to weigh yourself on a regular basis, I encourage you to speak with her/him about what you're working on, and why you'd like to discontinue this practice.

INTEGRATE:

1 For just one week to start, dispense of the scale habit. In its place, at your usual weigh-in time, sit down and take 3 deep breaths into your belly. Ask yourself, "What will weighing myself do for me right now?" Take your answer, and keep forging deeper. For example:

> • *Weighing myself right now will help me feel safe, because I'll know if I've gained weight and need to be "good" today.*
> • *How does my weight have anything to do with my being "good"?*
> • *Because if I'm fat I'm not good enough.*
> • *Good enough for what? For whom?*

Don't let yourself off the hook on this one. Keep pushing through to the next question until you get to the root of what the scale-number does for you.

It may be a lack of trust in yourself. It could be that someone in your life is asking you (even silently) to lose weight. It may be avoidance of something important trying to get your attention.

2 The next time you reach for a beauty or fitness magazine, pause and breathe. Consider how you'll feel after reading it. Be brutally honest here. Notice how it feels to see the 'perfect' model on the cover. Is there a sinking feeling in your gut? A little voice inside comparing your body to hers? If so, can you get angry at this media manipulation, instead of your body? See if you can walk away without buying or even reading the magazine any further. Notice the empowerment you feel from taking charge. Find an interesting alternative to read, unrelated to changing your body.

3 Begin to notice how often you check your reflection. Gradually build a new habit:

ignoring mirrors and windows. This may feel very vulnerable. When you've relied on your reflection to tell you you're okay (or not), it can feel pretty scary to become (and believe) your own voice of reassurance. Practice your deep breaths and keep trying. See if you can focus on areas other than your looks...like your wit, ability to empathize and be a good friend, or your skills and abilities on the job. Since you won't be visually observing your body, *feel* it instead: the strength of your legs as you stride down the sidewalk, the sensation in your arms as you wrap your kids or partner in a bear hug, the kiss of a soft breeze on your face. Your body is about so much more than its appearance. Start enjoying the full experience!

_____

_____

_____

_____

_____

_____

_____

_____

_____

_____

_____

_____

_____

_____

_____

_____

_____

_____

_____

_____

_____

_____

_____

_____

_____

_____

_____

_____

_____

_____

_____

_____

_____

_____

_____

_____

_____

_____

Chapter 13

BE MINDFUL OF
SWITCHING ADDICTIONS

BE MINDFUL OF SWITCHING ADDICTIONS

My dad passed away as I finished the final draft of this book. His gradual decline over several years had fooled me into thinking I was somewhat prepared for his death. Anyone who has lost someone close to them knows preparation isn't really possible.

I discovered that, even after many years of healing work, old addictive patterns will quietly sidle back into place during a crisis, snuggling in like a pair of comfy sweats; so easy and familiar; you hardly notice you're wearing them.

Such was the case after my father died. I went on high food alert; paying extra attention to my hunger and satiety signals. I moderated my indulgence in trigger foods, and enjoyed only an occasional glass of wine. I fed my body an abundance of water and fresh vegetable juices. I thought I was doing pretty well, considering the circumstances.

One day, about a month in, I noticed all my pants were feeling uncomfortably snug. My initial reaction, although brief, was a familiar cocktail of panic, paralyzing fear, and self-flagellating thoughts.

Cue body-love practice:

Pause.

Deep, nourishing belly breaths.

Loving reassurance: "It's going to be okay. I love you.

You're just trying to cope with something really hard."

Honest inventory: "What am I doing differently to make my body add weight?"

I knew food wasn't the lone culprit this time. Something else had changed, and when the answer came, it was forehead-smacking obvious: Netflix!

I had overlooked a vital step on this healing path: managing the tendency to switch addictions. Although I now manage emotional eating very well, traces of a deeply buried belief obviously remain: *it's dangerous to feel this much, too fast.* My psyche shifted into protective gear, quickly finding another way to stay safely numb.

I had to recognize and own my new form of binging: hours of watching one Netflix episode blur into another. I had also used the winter weather as an excuse to stop exercising. My lack of activity and hours of sitting were taking an obvious toll, manifesting in weight gain. It wasn't my body's fault; it responded appropriately to a heaping helping of inactivity and mind-numbing television. Perhaps most damaging of all, I had chosen numbness over feeling the incredible vulnerability of grief.

I know the word "addiction" can be loaded with preconceived judgments, and it's hard to admit being in its clutches. This is where courage and honesty make a repeat appearance. Healing can't happen in the midst of denial and avoidance. Take a deep breath and have a look...are you using any substance, activity, person, attitude or thing to distract, cope, or avoid? When you get a handle on one thing, like food, do you unwittingly search for a replacement?

Let's be clear...An occasional Netflix binge on a favorite show can be really fun! It becomes a problem (and blocks your healing) when it's used to avoid life. Losing yourself in anything external (Netflix, food, alcohol, shopping, gossip or sex, for instance) won't make the tough stuff disappear. Emotions simply nestle in for the duration, waiting for you to return and give them their due.

INTEGRATE:

So, you've switched your addiction from food to something else. The practice remains the same:

1 Get honest.
What's your new avoidance mechanism?

2 Sit with the cravings and temptation to lose yourself in this new practice.

3 Make a choice, without judgment:
binge or feel.

4 If you do binge, feel the effects fully. For instance, a TV binge brings me lethargy, depression, isolation, sadness, heaviness in body and spirit, and stiff muscles.

5 Find moderation. If your new avoidance-of-choice isn't destructive (e.g., gossip, anger, or an

unprotected/unhealthy sexual encounter), can you enjoy without excess?

6 Play. Move. Get your blood pumping. Laugh.

7 Take care of yourself. Where do you need nurturing? Where do you need to say "no", or "not right now"?

8 Make time for stillness, perhaps even allowing emotions to surface as you do. Welcome it all.

9 Encourage and support your body and spirit with lots of loving self-talk.

10 Be aware of any tendency to punish or control your body through measuring tools or comparison to false images of beauty.

_____

_____

_____

_____

_____

_____

_____

_____

_____

_____

_____

_____

_____

_____

_____

_____

_____

_____

_____

_____

_____

_____

_____

_____

_____

_____

_____

_____

_____

_____

_____

_____

_____

_____

_____

_____

_____

_____

_____

_____

_____

_____

Chapter 14

LATHER, RINSE, REPEAT

LATHER, RINSE, REPEAT

W*hatever we plant in our subconscious mind and nourish with repetition and emotion will one day become a reality.*

~Earl Nightingale

Although I'm many years into my food and body recovery journey, I feel addicted to sugar for the crajillionth time. I can't believe I'm here again; this place where it's hard to care or think about anything else. My body and brain are depending on sweet treats to add some meaning. I feel physically unwell; my spirit held captive and my life reduced to incessant craving. This is a hallmark of addiction...

continued use of a drug of choice, in spite of the adverse consequences it brings. It's time for a change, which I equally dread and welcome. Once this drug is out of my system, I'll feel fully alive and ready to pursue things that really matter. Sugar is a distraction, keeping me from my Best Self. I feel ready for a full dive into the soothing waters of my soul's purpose, and I know sugar holds me back. So, I practice. I feel the itchy craving, love myself, abstain from my drug and await the healing balm of time. Repeat and learn, repeat and grow, repeat and heal...a bit more each time.

While writing this book, I found myself with increased craving and food obsession. Because I'm exposing my secrets to the world (Getting honest, Chapter 4), my ego is nervous. It's reacting in its usual manner...use food for distraction, to avoid vulnerability and stay safe in what's familiar. My reaction? Notice, feel, reassure, and love myself (Chapter 5, Feel the craving). And, mindfully eat a little chocolate sometimes (Chapter 8, Find moderation). This isn't a practice of perfection, no matter how long you travel this road. The difference, over time, is in the amount you'll choose to consume, and in your level of motivation to make conscious, healthy behavior choices.

The other difference? You'll settle into a comfortable relationship with your body, with no desire to fix or change anything about it. Your decisions and choices stem from a deep respect and appreciation for all your body does for you.

If only we could complete the practices, check them off the list, and then simply move on, journey completed! But, we all know better. Life will continue pushing our vulnerability buttons, and food will always be a convenient and familiar path of avoidance. The good news...you get unlimited opportunities to practice your new strategies for handling difficulties as they arise.

Over time, the practices become intuitive, and your new normal.

This is not a linear process. Be ready to jump around a bit, depending on what issue seems most pressing on a given day. Revisit any practice as often as you need, keeping in mind some will feel easier than others. Be sure to work at all of them over time. Expect to flounder at times, and stand victorious at others. Just remember...floundering brings valuable lessons, which lead to later victories!

An important note: If you notice you're feeling an aversion to and avoiding some parts of the work, hit pause and take a deep breath. Anytime you start to think, "I don't need that" or "That doesn't apply to me," you're being given important information. Consider the distinct possibility you're bumping up against your shadow (Chapter 7). Whatever you resist is begging for compassionate attention. It may hold your most helpful and important lesson. Garner your courage, and give it a chance to be your greatest teacher.

Each time you courageously set food aside and welcome your emotions, you gain a firmer foundation for this healthier home you're building...a body that is cherished and appreciated by the only person that matters on this intimately personal journey...you.

Again, the Truth serving as the foundation of this food and body journey, and the one you must integrate if you want to heal:

You will make positive, lasting changes in your body when (and only when) you love yourself unconditionally.

This book is your get out of jail card...the jail of food anguish and body hatred. Revel in this thought!

Instead of the grueling effort to change yourself through diet and exercise, you get to love and nurture your body, allowing healthy changes to happen intuitively and organically.

Remember, harvest a powerfully-protective sense of self-love. Your well-being depends on it. Get angry at the dishonest, misleading and abusive messages about women's beauty and worth. Allow no one to disparage you or your body any longer.

A former client's story beautifully illustrates this practice in action:

"I went to get a haircut yesterday, and ran into someone I hadn't seen in a long time. She kept staring at my mid-section, which has thickened with this whole menopause thing, and which I'm very sensitive about. I walked out of the salon and that ferocious self-love you talk about kicked in. How DARE she, I thought. How DARE she stare, as if this remarkable body

is anything less than remarkable! I cannot be sure she was really looking at me that way, but that's how it felt. I loved the resistance and refusal I felt to grant her that permission, and also my refusal to join in her denigrating behavior."

It is my fervent hope and prayer for you, my brave partner on this journey, that your painful body relationship becomes one of peace, self-protection, compassion and wonder. May you also learn to eat with joy and mindful presence as a result.

Never forget that you are a beloved and Divine creation; not *after* you change yourself, but now and always.

_____

_____

_____

_____

_____

_____

_____

_____

_____

_____

_____

_____

_____

Lather, Rinse, Repeat

Lather, Rinse, Repeat

_____

_____

_____

_____

_____

_____

_____

_____

_____

_____

_____

_____

_____

References

Melody Beattie

Codepedent No More: How to Stop Controlling Others and Start Caring for Yourself (1987)

Hazelden; 1st edition

Brené Brown

Daring Greatly: How the Courage to Be Vulnerable Transforms the Way We Live, Love, Parent, and Lead

Avery; Reprint edition (April 7, 2015)

I Thought It Was Just Me (but it isn't): Making the Journey from "What Will People Think?" to "I Am Enough"

Avery (2007)

Pema Chodron

Getting Unstuck: Breaking Your Habitual Patterns and Encountering Naked Reality (2005)

Sounds True (audio)

Stephen Cope

Yoga and the Quest for the True Self (2000)

Bantam; 1 edition

Earon Davis

Quote downloaded from: http://www.livinglifefully.
com/moderation.htm

Used with author permission.

Charles Eisenstein

The Yoga of Eating: Transcending Diets and Dogma to
Nourish the Natural Self (2003)

Newtrends Publishing, Inc.; 2 Revised edition

Jonathan Fields

JonathanFields.com

Carl Jung

"Psychology and Religion" (1938). In CW 11: Psychology
and Religion: West and East. p.140

Ana Forrest *

Fierce Medicine: Breakthrough Practices to Heal the Body and Ignite the Spirit (2011)

HarperOne

Thomas Moore

Care of the Soul: How to Add Depth and Meaning to Your Everyday Life (1998)

Harper; 1st edition

Caroline Myss

Anatomy of the Spirit: The Seven Stages of Power and Healing (1996)

Harmony; 1 edition

Carolyn Gregoire

10 Ways Stress Affects Women (2013)

Downloaded from: http://www.huffingtonpost.com/2013/01/30/health-effects-of-stress-women_n_2585625.html

Donna Jackson Nakazawa

The Last Best Cure (2013)

Penguin Group USA, Inc.

Earl Nightingale

The Strangest Secret (2013)

Merchant Books

Christiane Northrup

Empowering Women's Health (2007)

Downloaded from: http://www.feminist.com/resources/

artspeech/health/empowering4.html

Mandy Oaklander

Time Magazine: The New Science of Exercise

Sep 12, 2016

Time.com

Don Henley and Stanley Lynch

Album, Hell Freezes Over (1994)

Marcelle Pick, NP

Weight Loss and Adrenal Stress (2017)

Downloaded from: https://www.womentowomen.com/

healthy-weight/weight-loss-and-adrenal-stress-2/

Gary Zukav

Soul to Soul: Communications From the Heart (2007)

Free Press Simon & Schuster, Inc.

Osho

Downloaded from http://www.osho.com/iosho/library

/library-search

*Not referenced but recommended

About the Author

Terri Leichty is a holistic health educator, coach, and mentor based in Boulder, Colorado. In addition to a social work degree, Terri has completed certification programs in wellness coaching, Kripalu Yoga, group fitness instruction, personal training, and an advanced health and fitness specialization.

With nearly 30 years of experience serving in a wide-variety of wellness, fitness, health care, and human services settings, Terri specializes in helping women heal from emotional eating and body image issues. From her personal journey of recovery from disordered eating and body hatred, Terri brings a uniquely empathetic perspective to the coaching process. Her wellness philosophy is about having fun, nurturing creativity, enjoying moderation, and harnessing the power of daily gratitude. She's ready to talk about a new brand of wellness... one not about deprivation, diets, or weight loss...but instead the joy, vitality, and improved health available through fierce, unconditional self-love.

Ready to dive deep and start your healing journey? Terri offers Body Love, Food Peace coaching for individuals and groups. Start the conversation at www.BodyLoveFoodPeace.com/Contact.

Made in the USA
Lexington, KY
16 September 2017